EVERYONE'S THE SMARTEST

First published in Great Britain in 2018 by the Emma Press
Originally published in 2015 as *Kõik on kõige targemad*

A CIP catalogue record of this book is available from the British Library

Supported by the Estonian Ministry of Culture

Printed in Latvia by Jelgavas tipogrāfija

ISBN 978-1-910139-99-8

THE EMMA PRESS LTD
Registered in England and Wales, no. 08587072
Website: theemmapress.com
Email: hello@theemmapress.com
Jewellery Quarter, Birmingham, UK

CONTRA EVERYONE'S THE SMARTEST

ULLA SAAR

Translated by Charlotte Geater
Kätlin Kaldmaa and
Richard O'Brien

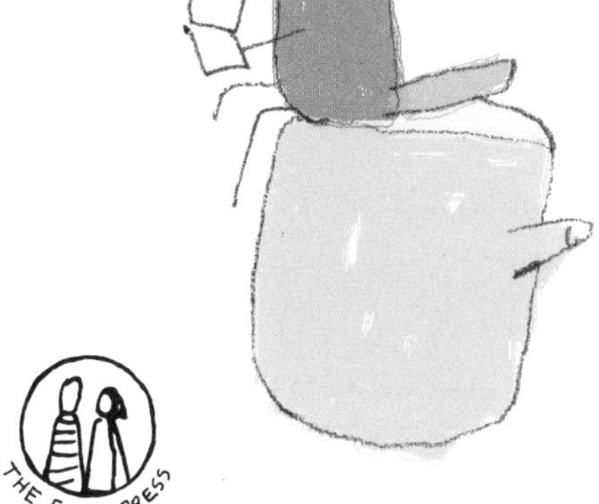

THE EMMA PRESS

CONTENTS

GOING TO SCHOOL (STEP, STEP, STOMP)

TOGETHER WE ARE STRONGER

MODERN DAY PINOCCHIO

SIXTEEN CHESS PIECES

TO READ AT THE SPEED OF A SQUIRREL

EVERYONE'S THE SMARTEST

BONUS BITS

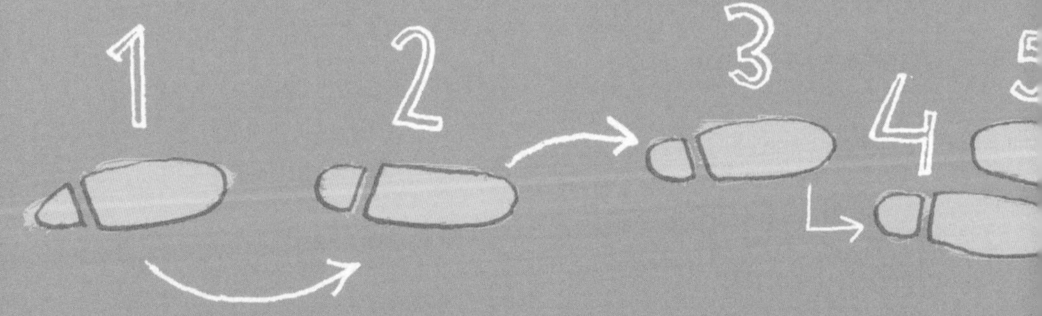
1
2
3
4

GOING TO SCHOOL (STEP, STEP, STOMP)

THE FIRST DAY OF SCHOOL

My shoes are brand-new
and this snow-white shirt too!
Now everybody: please make way –
a superhero started school today
whose test marks will go soaring
  through the roof.

THE FIRST WALK TO SCHOOL

'Hello, neighbours! Hi!!'

'Where are you going, dear child?'

'I'm going to school –
I already know all the letters!'

'But if you go abroad,
they might have different letters.'

'Luckily it's not that big, abroad,
and I'm sure I can also learn those letters.'

'But child, if you go to outer space
you'll find that they've got their own
whole set of letters.'

'Yes, space has lots more letters,
but I won't go too far –
If I choose one letter
as my favourite, I'll learn a lot
about just this
and when I write
I'll always leave
a lot of space
around it!'

NEW SCHOOL NIGHTMARE

I get to my new school –
it's fancy and big.

I've seen it before
but I don't think I saw
how scary it was, so huge –
so many mysterious rooms!

And the assembly hall's as wide
and noisy as a jungle –
beneath its hustle-bustle,
a tiger must be hiding!

Only my white shirt
can make my nerves calmer,
because I don't stand out –
the walls are magnolia!

I've already started praying
to be saved by the bell
when I hear with dismay
that my name's being called!

WAITING FOR THE SUMMER HOLIDAY

The summer sun's rays are sharp. I'm tired
of waiting for my first school-bell.
In September I start at the school down the road –
I couldn't go before, I was too small!

Right now, the big kids have their summer break
but I don't have any holiday at all –
before I can get my own, I have to wait
till I've finished a whole year of school.

GOING TO SCHOOL (STEP, STEP, STOMP)

Out of my bed [ahhhhh!]
getting dressed [rssshhh flup aarrggh ahh]
water from the tap [fssshhhhh ffssss hhhh rrsshh]
open the door [criiiiiiiik]
and then to school [step step stomp]
chalk on the blackboard [eeeeekk eeeee eeeeekkk!]

We are thinking [whirrr whirrrrr whirrrr]
the bell goes [BREEE ruuuussshhhh]
we run around [whirl HEY tap]
bigger boys louder [STOMP STOMP STOMP]
then run back home [ahh stomp step] ...

The day goes by so fast:
at night the Sandman scatters sand
in every little schoolchild's eyes
and gently scratches behind their ears.
I explore the land of sleep –
until the morning comes [cok-a-doodle-doo!]
the alarm clock is so loud [DRRIIIIIING]
breakfast is made [fzzzzzz fzzzzzz splat!]
going back to school [step stomp step]
until the day is gone again [tsuuhh-tsaauhh]

PINE CONES

In the morning I start off for school
half an hour early
and on the way I hide a little seed
in every hole in the street.

Right now my way to school is
cold and tough with tarmac
but one day, when my pines grow up....

I will walk my grandchildren to school
through a lovely forest,
and sometimes I will stop and pick
a cone for them.

A MAN IS NOT A FISH

I always have to walk to school,
but I'm not too upset:
I'd rather fly, but imagine if
I had to swim instead?
I'd rather walk than do front-crawl:
a man is not a fish.

MY SECRET PATH

From my house towards my school
I dug a secret way.
Fools who don't yearn for knowledge
only go there in the day.

But I will crawl like a mole
back to school every single night.
The tunnel starts beneath my bed:
buried out of sight!

Down the tunnel I slide, I sweep,
like water gushing from a tap.
I won't set off the burglar alarm:
it knows I don't mean any harm.

I skip from one classroom to the next,
fixing everything I see in my memory.
In the morning, in my bed
I wake up as a twice-as-clever me.

WAITING NERVOUSLY

My bed is harder than a rock,
I try and try, I can't drop off.

Tomorrow's something we can't miss:
a very important biology class.

My blanket's too warm for me to sleep –
it's like being cuddled by a sheep

I can't wait for tomorrow when
we're getting a visit from the Sandman.

No wait – it's not him after all.
Who grits the roads outside the school...

Ah, Mr Sand – he's visiting!
My legs have started counting sheep.
One is already in the land of sleep.

GOOD WORK!

TOGETHER WE ARE STRONGER

THE CARETAKER IS SCARED OF AUTUMN

The caretaker's afraid
of autumn most of all,
because there's always a parade
of dirty kids at school.

Because they love to jump
into the piles of leaves
and then they often stomp in mud
and get dirt on their knees.

The caretaker needs good luck
so that no colourful chump,

covered with autumn's muck,
ends up in the dump.

THE WONDROUS PLANT

In school we have a wonderful plant.
We help it grow. We all help out.

Each day a different year group
waters the soil around its roots.

Just yesterday, we had our chance
to water this amazing plant.

It's something I'm so glad about:
that we can help the plant to sprout,

and when it's time to pluck the fruit
there's nothing else for us to do.

Then the tomatoes will be our own:
we will eat what we have grown.

FISH AND CHIPS

I am very fast and keen,
sprinting down to the canteen,
I'm skipping every second step
because today, it's fish and chips.

Surely all children must love fish and chips!
We're so impatient, licking our lips.
Whenever I eat a feast this great,
I'm full of energy, I sit up straight
so I come top in every class!
My stomach purrs, contented as a well-fed cat.

HEALTHY INSIDE AND OUT

Our class is healthy,
and we think
it's all the milk
we like to drink.

The milk is just as good
for Tina as for Tim:
it's healthy to have fun
with everything.

KLARA AND SARA

In our class there's a
Klara, and a Sara.
What if they've switched?
Which one is which?

Their last names are
Klarnet and Sarnet.
Klara Sarnet
and
Sara Klarnet.

Klara and Sara,
Sara and Klara –
a person's name
is just an outline.

People can be called
any name at all,
but what matters is that
they are good at heart.

TOGETHER WE ARE STRONGER

When it's Independence Day
we raise our flag.
But the flag doesn't want to fly –
it sinks and sags.

That's why they make the whole school
line up smartly outside –
in case the flag falls down
we can blow until it flies.

ICE SKATER'S LAMENT

I'm miserable in winter –
I really want to skate,
but there's never been an ice-rink
within miles of my estate.

Sometimes outside my school
in the evening there's some ice,
glinting under moonlight –
a slice of paradise

but in the morning light
there's no sparkle to be found:
the Sandman every night
throws his grit on icy ground.

LET'S KEEP A SECRET

Santa Claus's furry coat
must be full of ten-pound notes.
He carries gifts like a donkey's pack;
only wants mince pies for payback.

Why do our mince pies
make him want to fly?
But we all love gifts,
getting presents from our lists,

so let's keep the secret: try
not to tell him that mince pies
are an easy thing to get
on the internet.

FANCY SKIS

After Christmas is finished
I can't wait to go to school.
All my friends are astonished –
my gifts were super cool.

I am so excited by
my super-duper skis,
I take them in to school –
feel like a celebrity.

They're for a trip in PE,
but when we're there I freeze,
because the teacher tells me
to ski on my new skis!

I've got to make it down the slope –
the others slide with ease,
and all I can do is hope
that I don't scratch my super skis!

SNOWBALL FIGHT

Real battles are ugly,
but a snowball war
definitely isn't!
Snow makes my heart soar.

Then I can throw ammo
as my classmates scream,
but I bet it's tasty –
mate, eat this ice cream!

SCARF PARTY

In windy winter weather,
I went to school without a scarf.
I was afraid they'd tease me –
call me 'Scarf Boy!' in front of the class.

For just one day, one single day,
I went to school without my scarf
but I'm paying for it now –
nothing's fun with this cough!

Now all I can do today is lie
on my sickbed, wrapped up warm.
I don't dare to go anywhere
without a scarf, even at home.

GLOVE

We went on a school trip to a grand
and beautiful foreign town.
On the way back (oh boy!) I suddenly found
I'd left my left glove behind.

I am secretly a little bit glad
that I forgot a glove,
because now I might get to go back
to that bustling town I loved!

PAPA C

MODERN DAY PINOCCHIO

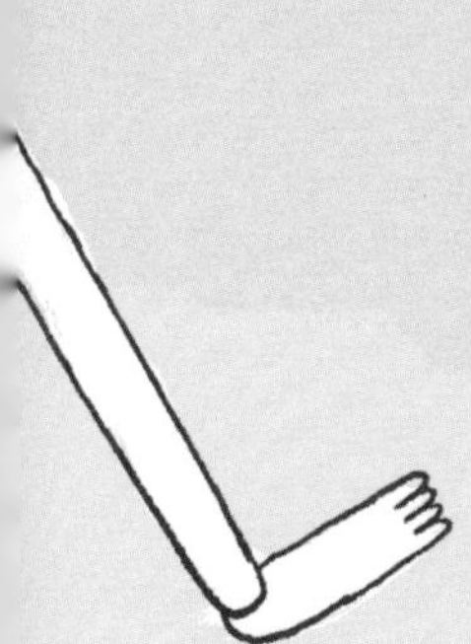

THE CLEVER DUCK

Behind the school there is a little park,
and in that park there lives a little duck.
Like all ducks are, this duck is very smart:
it knows when southerly migrations start;
the route it takes is right, the time is right,
and right on time, it makes its homeward flight.
The duck knows where it has to go without
going to school.
So why then do I have to study like a fool?
At every turn, this world's unjust and cruel!

RESTLESS RICHARD

My teacher told me off again:
'Richard, you're always rustling!
In class you need to sit up straight
and focus on the lesson!'

I won't waste time explaining
how I could've sat still without complaining
if there hadn't been a fly
trying hard to catch my eye.

MODERN DAY PINOCCHIO

I don't want to go to school,
I've never earned a penny there.
I'd rather sell my dictionary
and buy a combine harvester.

Then I'll jump proudly to the wheel,
pull some kind of lever,
and all day through I'll bravely toil
collecting crops and tubers,
then go to market, where I'll sell
and get more cash than ever.

And even when the winter comes,
I'll hop around like a magpie,
peeking under every stone,
hoping to find some money.

HUNGRY CAT

In our classroom the air was thick,
and at the bell the teacher said:
Let's not go to lunch. The cat

has clearly got all of your tongues –
nobody answered a question
in this whole lesson.

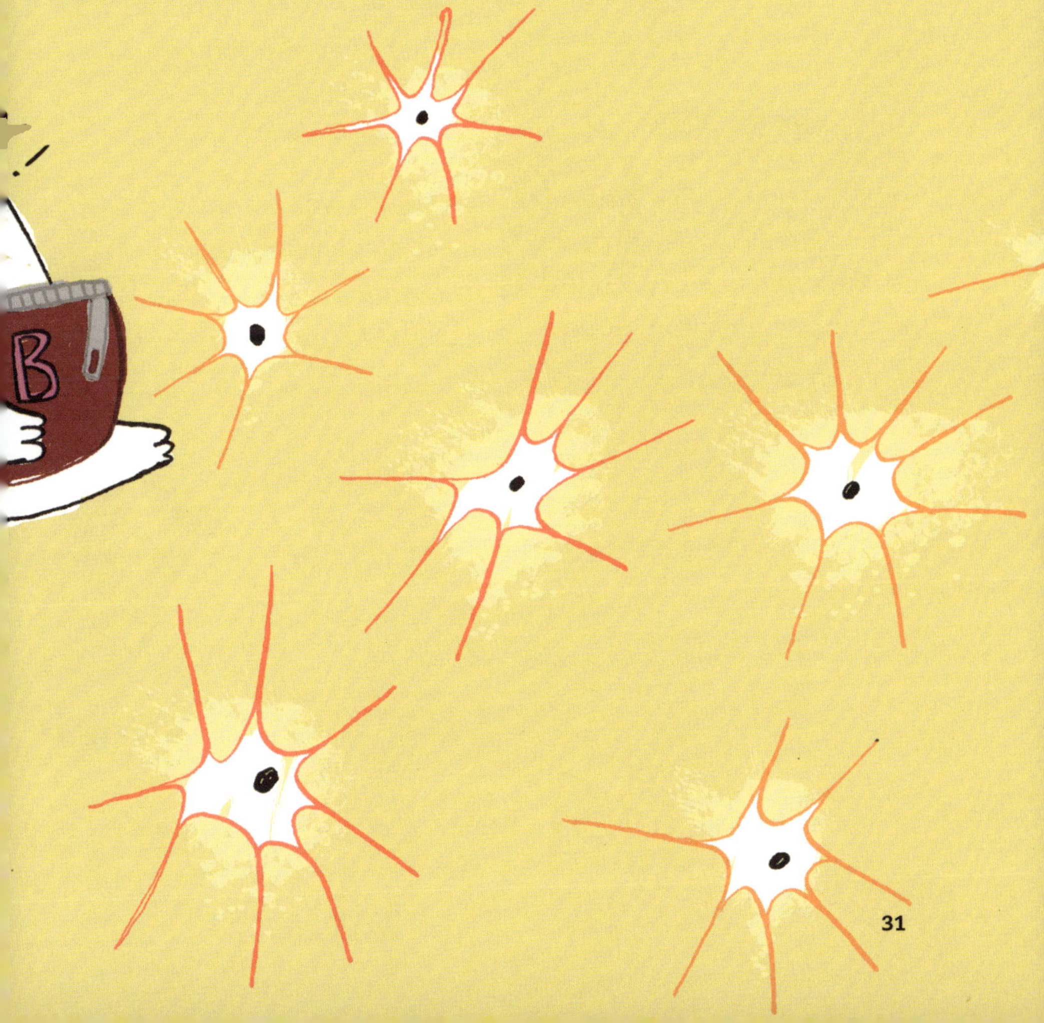

A QUESTION OF FUNDS

Whenever I've caused
some chaos at school,
my cashflow suffers
as a general rule,

because every time
that I get in a scrape,
my pocket-money
is taken away.

But if I was careful,
as good as an angel,
my parents' wallets
surely couldn't take it.

AN IMPORTANT GUEST

A traveller from abroad
came to our school one day.
By birth he was a Lord.
His glasses were pince-nez.

The dust that piled up high
was swept from all the floors.
They made us stand in one long line –
a line-up. That's the word.

The lord stood at the podium –
we all had to applaud.
He spoke at length, then off he rode
on horseback. Mighty lord!

And when this lord was gone,
all the children in a horde
ran wild. If children can't have fun
the rules are very flawed.

HURRY UP!

English lessons are annoying,
endless sentences to form...
Hurry up and finish!
I want to go out and run!

PE class is annoying,
they're always making us run...
Hurry up and finish!
I'm tired, I want to sit down!

There are a lot of points on which
our teachers should reflect –
why is it that they've picked
the wrong time for every subject?

SCRATCHING LESSONS

When your Mum has taken care
to sit you down and braid your hair
you can dance through break that morning
like a princess in a story.

But in class when thinking hard,
it helps to scratch your head.
That's when the unravelling starts –
thoughts as well as braids.

Days that start with well-made braids
have never ended well.
Why can't Scratching Class be made
compulsory at school?

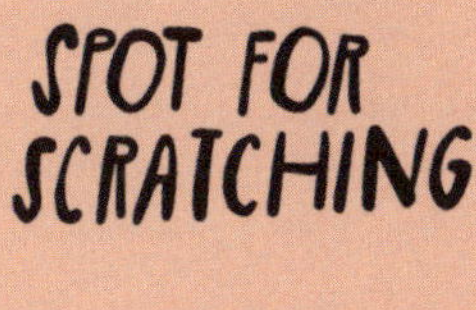

FIGHTING SLEEP

I'm already really sleepy
by the second class.
I would sleep till evening came
if they'd just let it pass.

But I wonder: could I ever
sleep the grown-up way?
Could I snore as nicely as
my teacher does all day?

SPRING PROBLEMS

Once again Alex was late
getting to his lesson;
our strict teacher Ms Braithwaite
asked him for a reason.

Yes, it's sadly true:
who among us is never late?
'I am only human,'
said my classmate.

Out in the shining sun,
the spring extends its arms.
On our way to school
it throws surprises in our path.

Sometimes there are rocks which dare us
to a game of footie.
Think of all the fun we could have
with these cute puppies!

Oh, all the things I'd see!
Oh, all the things I'd do!
In the spring we ought to have
more time to walk to school.

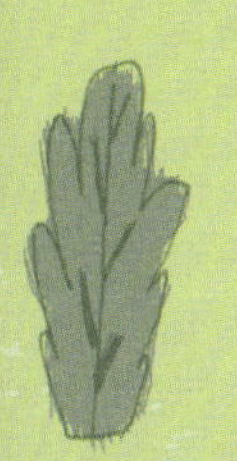

SUNBEAMS

Water drills tunnels in the snow,
the sun shines summer-bright,
and somehow it's both cold and hot outside.

Oh, how our classroom seems
suddenly so cramped and tight,
the windows are too small for all that sunlight.
Oh, how hard it is to sit and listen in my class today…
Let me ride on a sunbeam, far away!

FUTURE ARTISTS

1.A

In art lessons when we create
a mural or a sugar-paper chart,
the joy of crafting with classmates
plants a fertile seed of art.

Once we thought that the very paints
and pastels we adored
could surely be the thing to decorate
the classroom door.

Our glee lasted only a moment,
now our hearts are ill-at-ease –
we must scrub off, as punishment,
our immortal masterpiece.

SIXTEEN CHESS PIECES

IT'S NOT EASY TO BE A MONKEY

Children have this feeling –
we'd like to still be monkeys!
The blackboard's so appealing:
you could climb it like a tree.

But you can't just be left to hang
in monkey peace, and chill – a
teacher's always on your back,
as harsh as a gorilla.

KRISTJAN PALUSALU

Once there was a very famous wrestler
called Kristjan Palusalu,
and for his wrestling prowess
the president gave him a farmhouse.

One day I too will be a great man
like Kristjan Palusalu,
I will throw other boys my size around
like an otter flings little fish.

I will make my country proud
like Kristjan Palusalu,
but at school wrestling isn't allowed:
our headteacher can't stand violence.

He won't let me wrestle,
no matter how much I ask,
and this means I won't be successful
like Kristjan Palusalu.

CLASSMATE FUN

I really like the boy I sit next to,
the one called Robin –
it's fun to play with him,
because we have a lot in common.

Robin is very good at
shooting arrows
and I can run away,
fast as an arrow.

My friend and I
won't ever get bored, ever:
not when we spend all of our days
playing at elk and hunter.

Robin aims at my tail,
shrieking battle-cries.
Sometimes a shot will fail –
that's when I fly.

BREAKTIME FUN

At school we have a lot of fun,
when we're playing chase.
Yesterday Elina
fell right on her face.

Only today Lembit fell
and he got such a bump
it looked like the horn of a unicorn.
We have a lot of fun.

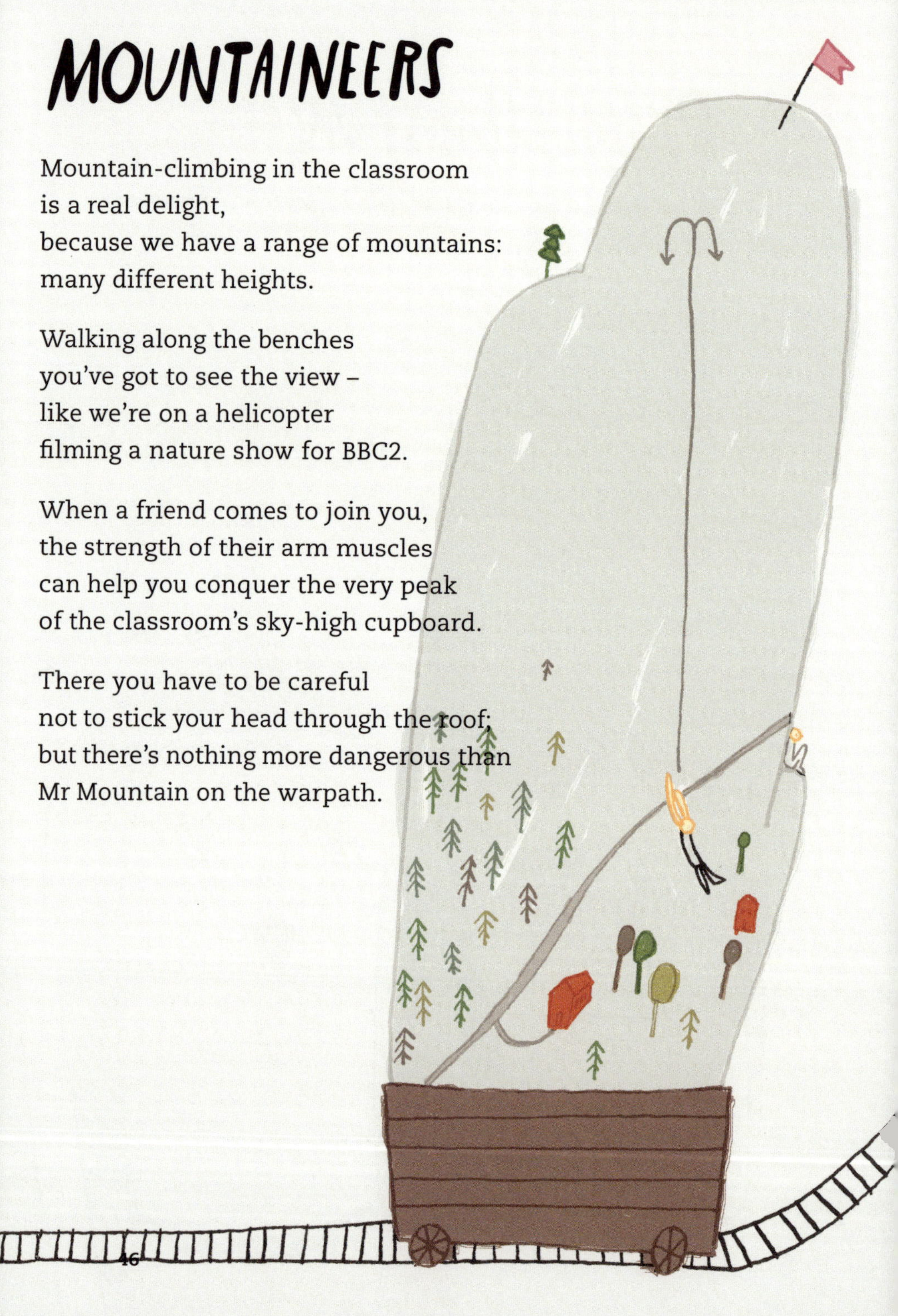

MOUNTAINEERS

Mountain-climbing in the classroom
is a real delight,
because we have a range of mountains:
many different heights.

Walking along the benches
you've got to see the view –
like we're on a helicopter
filming a nature show for BBC2.

When a friend comes to join you,
the strength of their arm muscles
can help you conquer the very peak
of the classroom's sky-high cupboard.

There you have to be careful
not to stick your head through the roof;
but there's nothing more dangerous than
Mr Mountain on the warpath.

ALIEN RAILWAY

Once upon a time the aliens
came to visit us:
I'll never forget the day they built
a railway in our class.

AlienRail goes under the roof,
so it doesn't distract our brains.
During break, if you dare, you can
ride up there
on the brand-new alien train.

SIXTEEN CHESS PIECES

With our teacher there are
exactly sixteen of us here.
Like sixteen chess pieces,
we all have the same hair.

Rocky – the rook – always wants
to rush on straight ahead.
But Christy is like the bishop,
only criss-crossing the board.

The teacher is the tallest of us all –
he is our king.
He rarely ventures outside his space.
He tends to do his own thing.

And Rav who never stays still
only walks around like a knight,
making his movements over our heads
like thunder on a stormy night.

FLOODING AT SCHOOL

This morning I arrived
to see quite a surprise.
Those used to be the stairs –
now there's water everywhere.

And water flows in front of me
like flickers on an old TV –
it's wet on every step...

Aha! I know what's up!
I think I understand:
somebody washed their hands
and didn't turn off the tap.

TO READ AT THE SPEED OF A SQUIRREL

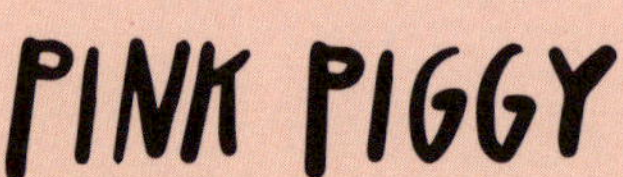

PINK PIGGY

At school we can't complain
that our days are filled with boredom.
Just now a pink piggy
flew across the classroom.

Kaitlin's brought in a balloon
like a pink pig on a string.
Now we're facing the school day smiling,
ready for anything.

A SPEEDY SNAIL

I don't really feel
in the mood for fun today;
the snail I brought to school with me
escaped and got away.

I was patiently learning
fractions,
while the snail was racing,
dashing.

Even if I'm quick and
chase after its trail,
it's impossible to catch
a turbo racing snail.

SPORTS DAY: GOOD NEWS AND BAD NEWS

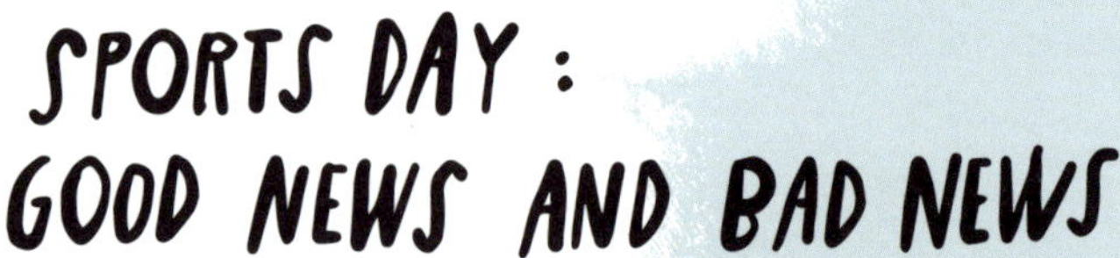

During sports day
we ran long-distance;
I was the fastest –
... I ran past the finish.
I have to admit this.
It's really a shame.
Another runner won. My run
was just for fun and games.

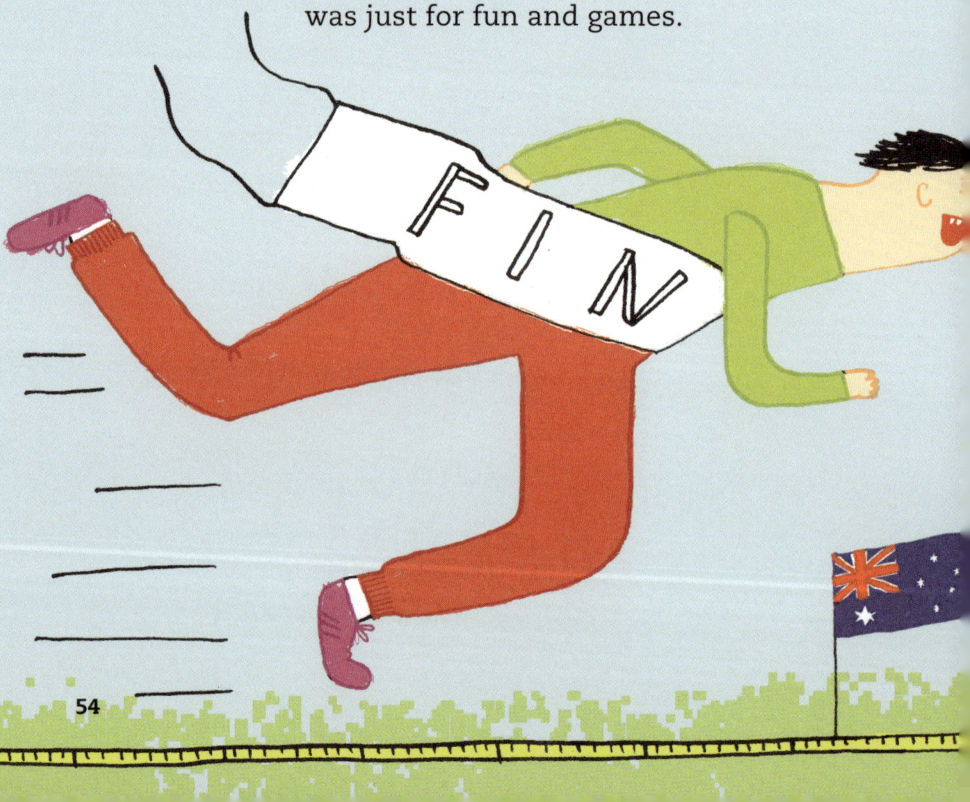

EXCHANGE STUDENT

I didn't believe
that our school really
had an exchange student
over from Sydney,

because they don't even
walk upside down
and I've seen their belly:
there isn't a pouch.

But now I can call them Australian
without any further to-do,
because I've seen them do the high-jump
like a kangaroo.

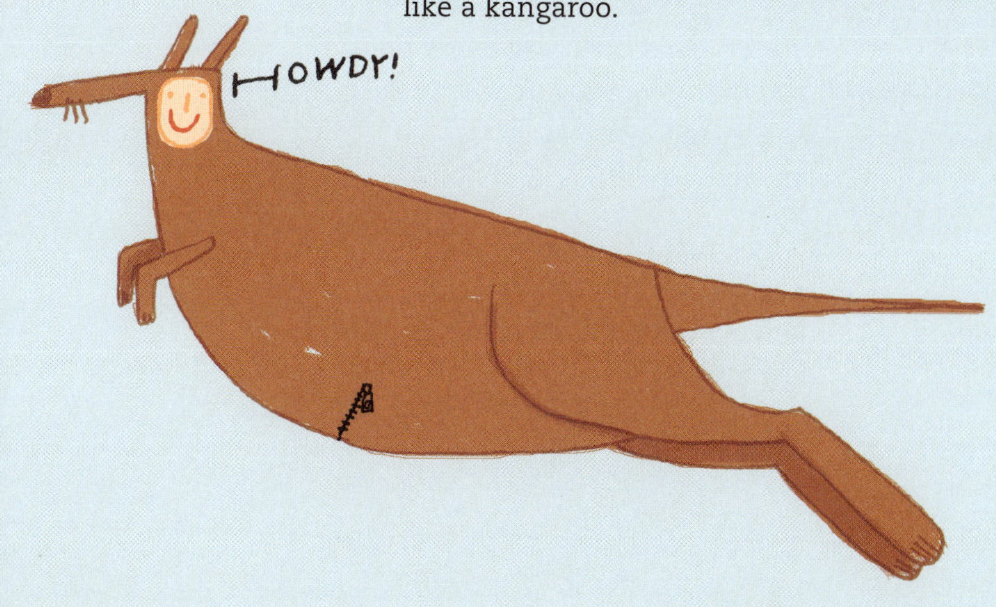

FIRST IN THE CLASS!

I always try my hardest
to be top of every class
and I want to arrive at school
before everyone else.

But my mum doesn't care,
she sleeps in far too late –
she's why I'll never make it
to school before half-eight.

One time we almost made it,
I was ready to rejoice –
but my Mum's driving went at a crawl,
as slow as a tortoise.

She stopped the car at every light,
and didn't move along –
she wasn't overtaking
anyone.

If I were at the wheel,
you can bet I'd race and spin
and get there fifteen minutes before
anyone else walked in.

BIGGER OR SMALLER?

In PE we're told
to do lots of sports
to make our bodies
big and strong.

But my dad gets told
to do more sport
to make his belly smaller –
something's wrong.

CLEVER DAD

Dad did really well at school,
he only got top marks.
Mum must be so proud of him,
she listens and she laughs.

DADDY

READING: 5
WRITING: 5
MATHEMATICS: 3+2

A CRUCIAL CLOTH

Back in the day a blackboard wipe
had a lot of chalk to clean off:
the world moves on, and now's a time
with little use for the cloth.

But even now a tablet
often needs a wiping clean;
unless you fancy picking dust-motes
one by one off the screen.

MY PET

Yesterday Lisa brought to school
a sweet but lazy
tiny fuzzy
cat.
Our teacher told us cats
are not suited to the classroom,
and that was
that.
Tomorrow I would like to go
to school with my cuckoo-clock.
I love my pretty cuckoo:
how smartly it sits in its box!

Cuckoo knows all the numbers,
so well it could go to college.
But it still has lots to learn.
Cuckoo only knows one word
which is insufficient knowledge.

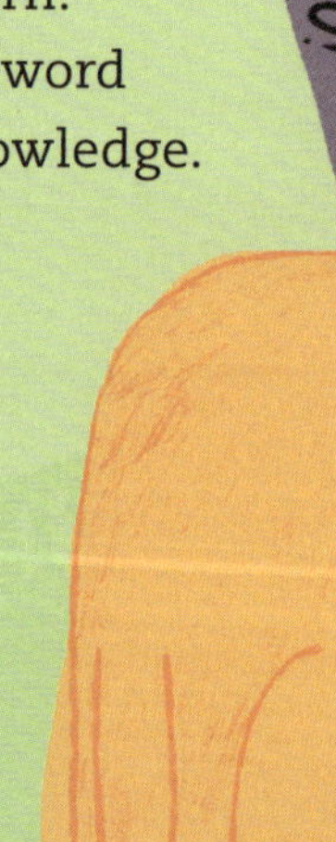

MY TEACHER IS A SQUIRREL

Clever squirrel, beneath the window,
dashing across a tree –
you'd beat us in a climbing race, I know
– so can't you teach us to read?'

I suppose it would be silly to read
as fast as our squirrel climbs.
You could certainly read at a sprinting speed
... but without understanding a line.

EVERYONE'S THE SMARTEST

A WILFUL POEM

A bad poem doesn't want
to stick in my head.
I can only remember a little bit,
so I turn to the book instead.

Why does this evil poet
write such awful poems?
Why do they need to bully
little human beings?

Stop right there, poet!
Although I'm smaller than you
I'll learn this poem off by heart
even better than you could do.

HOW I LEARNED A AND O

I took hold of an ABC
and learned the A like a recipe.
Now I feel like pizza:
they can roll the fancy dough
until it's big and round just like an O.

MATHS

I really liked doing adding up,
because the best at Maths can win a cup.
But I didn't like the subtracting part –
I thought it would get me a negative mark.

So I took care to only add up,
but it didn't get me an A++,
just a C with a long minus –

Now I've learnt you can use a minus
for taking numbers off,
and that it won't get you a telling-off.

MATH-SMARTS

Yesterday evening was very busy:
we had a lot to do, me and my friend,
so though we had a test, we didn't study,
but we still got ten out of ten.

But why did the teacher have to divide
the mark up between us, in half?
My friend got a five and I got a five,
so now we're both getting told off.

I'll give my marks to my friend: with the scores
added up, they can ace the whole test.
That way I'll have nothing to get told off for,
and they'll get praised for being the best.

MUSIC TEACHER

Dear Ms Horne, do you know
how much is four times four?

Or do you only know how to magic
sound out of a horn,
how to write music notation,
how to tell stories in the middle
of a keyboard demonstration?

I'm sure you know a lot, but if
you'd really rather not do maths
do not fear, dear Ms Horne,
I'll tell you myself
how much is four times four.

CLASS ORCHESTRA

All of us are true musicians,
and we have cool instruments –
Brrrring, Lalala
Ring Ring, Blip
Bleeeeep, DaDaDaDaDaaaaa
Ping!, Dobeedo

Every instrument has its own song
and our teacher is the singer –
usually she sings a single line
which we know like a classic banger:
'Turn off your phones!'

QUEEN

Our school is a big palace,
at the end of a tree-lined street,
even our classroom
feels like a castle,
because we are taught
by a queen.

Perhaps I need to explain
why we call our teacher
the queen?

Well it's perfectly clear:
our year is the oldest year
so it would be obscene
to be taught by anyone
except a queen.

THE SMARTEST TEACHER

I like to go to school,
and I'm never late for classes,
because of our wonderful teacher:
Mr Markus.

Wisdom flows out of his mouth
like molten gold that sparkles.
Every morning – I know it's true –
he drives into school from Harku.

I believe that Mr Markus
has a magic park in Harku
where he waters trees and plants that
grow up full of all the answers.

EVERYONE'S THE SMARTEST

In our class the kids are smart,
our heads are full of clever thoughts.
Some of us know a lot about chess,
some about kicking a ball in the net,
some are quick at mental maths,
some at walking really fast,
some are great at eating pies,
some are good at telling lies.
You won't find a class that's better than our class is,
where everybody all agrees
that everyone's the smartest.

WHO MADE THIS BOOK? LET'S FIND OUT...

ABOUT THE POET

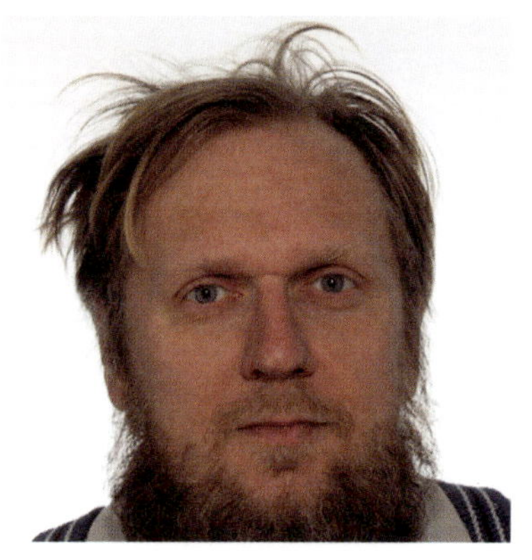

Contra (born Margus Konnula in 1974) is one of Estonia's most prolific contemporary poets. Since his debut in 1995, he has published at least one poetry collection each year.

Contra's writing is strongly rooted in Estonia's contemporary folk-singing tradition, with gleeful and witty texts that blend dense, playful rhymes with topical issues. Contra's poetry stands out for the frequent use of his native Võru dialect, and he is a popular guest on television, at public events, and in schools.

Contra is a laureate of the Oskar Luts Prize for Humor and the Bernard Kangro Award for Literature; in 2015 he was awarded the Estonian Cultural Endowment's Award for Children and Youth Literature.

ABOUT THE ILLUSTRATOR

Ulla Saar (1975) is an illustrator, product designer, graphic artist, and interior designer.

She graduated from the Estonian Academy of Arts in product design, and currently works as a designer.

Her first illustrated book, *Lift*, immediately received widespread recognition, and was listed in the 2014 White Ravens catalogue by the International Youth Library. Since then, Ulla has illustrated nearly 20 books, every one of which has gained international attention.

Ulla practices a contemporary, design-like approach to book illustration: her spirited and playful art is often more a part of the book's overall design than free-standing pictures.

Photo: Joonistan Hobuveskit

ABOUT THE TRANSLATORS

Kätlin Kaldmaa is an Estonian poet, writer, translator and literary critic. She has published four collections of poetry (*Larii-laree, One is None, Worlds, Unseen* and *The Alphabet of Love*), two children's books, a novel (*No Butterflies in Iceland*), and a short story collection (*The little sharp knife*).

Her poetry has been translated into more than 20 languages and her collections have been published in English, Finnish and Spanish. She has written extensively on literature and translated more than 80 works of world's best literature. In 2012 she won the annual Friedebert Tuglas short story award.

Kätlin Kaldmaa is the International Secretary of PEN International. She is currently working on her fifth collection of poetry and on her second novel.

Photo: Toomas Volmer

Charlotte Geater is a poet and editor based in London, UK.

She has a PhD in Creative Writing from the University of Kent. She edits children's poetry and fiction for the Emma Press, and poetry for adults too.

Her own writing has been published by *Queen Mob's Teahouse, Galley Beggar, Strange Horizons* and *The Best British Poetry 2013*.

Richard O'Brien is a poet, translator and academic based in Birmingham, UK.

His co-translations, all from Latvian, include: for children, *The Noisy Classroom* (Ieva Flamingo) and *The Book of Clouds* (Juris Kronbergs); for adults, *Narcoses* (Madara Gruntmane). He is a commissioning editor at the Emma Press and has a PhD on Shakespeare and the development of verse drama.

In 2017, he won an Eric Gregory Award from the Society of Authors for his own poetry.

Photo: Jack Spicer Adams

NOW FOR SOME

BONUS BITS

INTERVIEW WITH CONTRA

When did you start writing poems?

15 years old, in my first year at secondary school.

Do you remember the first poem you wrote?

My first poem was called 'Why didn't we achieve Communism?' The short answer was: too much vodka.

What was your favourite subject at school?

At school I was very lazy (that's why I'm not very highly educated) but I always read books. I guess my favourite subject was Literature. From the books on the syllabus, I most liked *Catcher in the Rye* and *Faust*.

Which is your favourite illustration in this book?

The illustrations in this book are more just than illustrations: every picture works and breathes together with the poem and I feel every illustration works as an extra verse of its poem. As for my favourite – maybe the one for 'Class Orchestra' (page 69).

What advice would you give to a budding poet?

Everyone should try to write poems – if you and your friends like it, it's already a success. If you want to become a great Poet, first you have to love poetry and to read lot of good poetry in different styles. Also read bad poetry, because then you will find out which poems you don't want to write. And then try to write a poem which nobody has written yet.

INTERVIEW WITH ULLA

How did you become an illustrator?

By working hard and being determined.

What advice would you give someone who wants to be an illustrator?

Work hard. Develop your own style. Be determined.

Which are your favourite poems in this book?

'Klara and Sara' (page 18), and 'The smartest teacher' (page 71)

Can you tell us the story behind one of your illustrations?

When I was at school, during the Soviet times, most janitors wore specific buttoned coats with big pockets. They could be either deep blue or brown (the coats, not pockets) but I mostly remember them as blue. That's why the janitor on page 14 ended up wearing a blue coat. It probably won't make much sense to kids nowadays!

What projects are you working on at the moment?

I just finished illustrating a translation of Norton Juster's *The Phantom Tollbooth* and in the beginning of September I'm going to start to illustrate a book about a girl who's starting school. In Estonia children start school at 7; before that they go to kindergarten.

What's your favourite thing to draw?

People.

LEARN SOME ESTONIAN

We've picked out some words that were in the original Estonian poems, along with how to say them (in brackets). Roll your *rrr*s, and pronounce Ks a tiny bit like Gs, and Ps a tiny bit like Bs.

- **school** .... **kool** (gawwl)
- **teacher** .... **õpetaja** (HUP-eh-tie-ah)
- **milk** .... **piim** (peeeem)
- **caretaker** .... **koristaja** (COR-ees-tie-ah)
- **breaktime** .... **vahetund** (VAR-had-weend)
- **classroom** .... **klass** (klassss)
- **famous cool pink skis** ...... **kuulsad tuusad roosad suusad** .... (gAWWL-zer tAWW-zad *rrr*AWW-zad tsAWW-zad)
- **ice-skating** .... **uisutamine** (WOI-zer-tam-in-a)
- **snow** .... **lumi** (low-mee)
- **cat** .... **kass** (kusss)
- **kangaroo** .... **känguru** (KANG-uh-*rr*oh)
- **puppy** .... **kutsikas** (kOU-tsik-as)
- **squirrel** .... **orav** (o*rrr*-av)
- **snail** .... **tigu** (tig-aww)
- **sun** .... **päike** (pie-keh)

PLACES IN ESTONIA

Tallinn

The capital city of Estonia. It has a beautiful walled medieval centre, built around two streets leading up to a castle. These two streets are called Pikk Jalg and Lühike Jalg, which mean 'long leg' and 'short leg'!

The Estonian Children's Literature Centre

A beautiful storybook building on a magical cobbled street in Tallinn's Old Town. It has a library of children's books, a Fairytale Attic, galleries filled with art, and is home to the Children's Book Museum. Visitors can learn about the Centre's mascot, Nukitsamees (that's 'Bumpy' in English), and once a week young readers can practice their reading with the centre's most important staff members – the reading dogs!

Harku

A small town in northern Estonia, just to the west of the capital Tallinn. It has lighthouses, waterfalls, and a historic manor house where in 1710 a treaty was negotiated making Estonia part of the Russian empire. Harku is the town Mr Markus comes from in the poem 'The Smartest Teacher' (page 71).

Other favourite places in Estonia

Ulla: I've always liked the beach in north-east Estonia called **Aa**.

Kätlin: **Käru**, aka (literally) Wheelbarrow – a place where my grandma used to live when I was a child.

Contra: **Rüä** has a great name, and my home is in **Urvaste**.

WRITE YOUR OWN POEM!

Fancy writing your own poem and then maybe illustrating it too? Translators Richard O'Brien and Charlotte Geater have come up with some ideas to help get you started.

What do you see on **your journey to school**? What do you hear, and smell? What do you wish was there? Write a poem about your ideal morning journey to school.

What's **your favourite meal or snack** to eat at school? Is it fish and chips (like on page 16) or something else? Do you like spaghetti or are you always keen to eat a flapjack? Write about how you feel when you think about this food – and see if you can think of words that rhyme with the food!

Take a look at 'Scratching lessons' on page 35. What **new kinds of classes** do you wish there were at school? Would you like to learn to grow taller, or to talk to your pet dog? Write down what you would like to learn and why!

'Kristjan Palusalu' (page 43) is about a wrestler who is very famous in Estonia. **Pick a person who you think is important or impressive** and write a poem where you contrast your life with their life. Maybe you want to drive a racing car like Lewis Hamilton, but right now you're just about to take your cycling proficiency test... Try to repeat the person's name once in every verse.

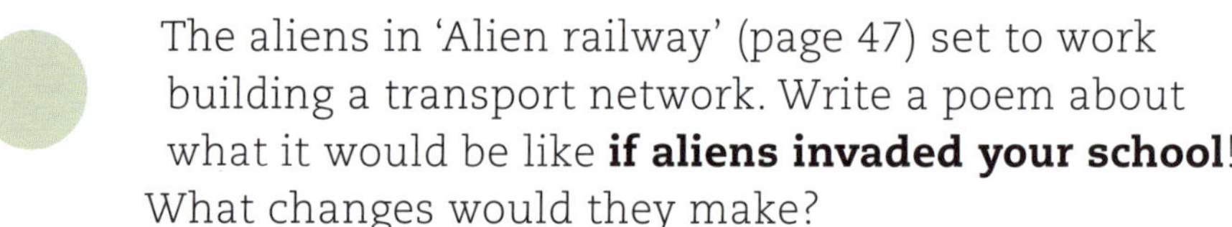

The aliens in 'Alien railway' (page 47) set to work building a transport network. Write a poem about what it would be like **if aliens invaded your school**! What changes would they make?

In 'Math-smarts' (page 67), the speaker uses some dodgy logic to claim that they got ten out of ten in a test. Think of a subject you study, and list some of the things you have to do in that class.

Now **imagine you've got in trouble and you want to make your teacher see your side of things**. How could you use some of these ideas from school to make your own clever argument? Think especially about the way Contra is being cheeky with the truth in his poem. Here are some lines you could use to start off:

'In my defence, you said to kick the ball...'
'I didn't make the rules of Chemistry...'
'It's not my fault recorders make that noise...'

Write a poem which has sounds at the end of every line, like 'Going to school (Step Step STOMP)' on page 6. Think about the sound of everything that you're writing about! What does it sound like when you're writing in your exercise book, or when you're playing outside?

We'd love to see what you come up with in response to these prompts! If you'd like us to take a look, email your poems and pictures to hello@theemmapress.com **with 'Everyone's the Smartest' in the subject line.**

TRANSLATION STATION

Contra's poems are full of rhymes and jokes and fun with words in the original Estonian. One of the biggest challenges for the three translators – Charlotte, Kätlin and me (Richard) – was to recreate all the fun and joy in the English versions.

But sometimes translation is about more than just the words. Throughout *Everyone's the Smartest*, **we found ideas that were very specific to school and life in Estonia. We wanted to make the poems clear for you to read in English, but sometimes that meant we had to replace Estonian references with English ones.**

This section gives you a sneak peek behind the scenes of the translation process. If you're a budding translator, you can use it to think about our work – would you have made the same choices? If you have ideas or questions about translating, we'd love to hear from you by email: hello@themmapress.com**.**

On page 16, the child in the poem is 'sprinting down to the canteen' to get their favourite food: 'fish and chips'. But the title of the original poem in Estonian is '**minced meat sauce**' – this is a popular meal with beef and gravy, served with fresh dill.

The illustrator Ulla told us that minced meat sauce is 'very non-illustration friendly'. She didn't want to just draw a 'grey blob', so 'finally I ended up drawing a kid running towards the sauce instead,' she says – and luckily this illustration works for fish and chips just as well!

On page 10, the person visiting the school in 'Waiting nervously' is not 'Mr Sand', but **Mati Kaal** – he is a real man, famous in Estonia as a former director of the Tallinn Zoo.

We thought about who in the UK might be well-known for similar reasons: TV nature presenters like Chris Packman or Bill Oddie came to mind, but their names didn't work with the joke about the Sandman. One translator even suggested Sandi Toksvig! ... but ultimately we decided 'Mr Sand' just made the most sense.

In our version of 'Modern day Pinocchio' (page 30), the child leaves school to buy a combine harvester and sell potatoes. In Contra's version, they buy **a snowplough** to sell snow at the market.

Estonia gets more snow than the UK, and we thought this might sound too strange as an idea! But all translation is about making choices, and sometimes we wonder if we should have kept it strange rather than trying to make it normal. What do you think? What would you have done?

'Hungry cat' (page 31) is a poem based around the English phrase 'the cat has got your tongue.' This is totally different to the actual words used in Estonian, because in the original language there is a phrase about being annoying, saying **the children have eaten the teacher's nerves**. That didn't work in English, but we've kept the original picture to tell some of the same story.

In 'Together We Are Stronger' (page 19), schoolchildren line up to celebrate **Independence Day**. This is an important holiday in Estonia.

In fact, there are two Independence Days: one on 24th February celebrates the Estonian Declaration of Independence in 1918, and a second on 20th August marks the Restoration of Estonian Independence, after the fall of the Soviet Union in 1991. At first we thought we should find an English equivalent, like St George's Day, but here we decided it was important to keep the meaning of the original.

• • •

'Let's keep a secret' (21) features the age-old link between Santa Claus and mince pies. But in fact this is our English version of what's happening: the Estonian tradition, as described in the original poem, is that **children have recite a poem – or sing a song – to Santa in exchange for every present they receive**.

There are traditional poems which many children know by heart for the occasion – but if they're feeling creative, they might also write their own. After reading our prompts on the previous pages, maybe you'll be doing the same this Christmas!

• • •

ABOUT THE EMMA PRESS

The Emma Press is a publishing house based in Birmingham, UK. It makes books for adults and children, and specialises in poetry.

Emma Press books are starting to win prizes, including the Poetry Book Society Pamphlet Choice Award and the Saboteur Award for Best Collaborative Work. Having been shortlisted for the Michael Marks Award for Poetry Pamphlet Publishers in both 2014 and 2015, the Emma Press finally won it in 2016 (hurray!).

Falling Out of the Sky: Poems about Myths and Monsters, the first Emma Press poetry book for children, was shortlisted for the 2016 CLiPPA, run by the Centre for Literacy in Primary Education. *Moon Juice* , a collection of poems by Kate Wakeling with illustrations by Elīna Brasliņa, won the CLiPPA in 2017.

You can find out more about the Emma Press and buy books directly from us here:

theemmapress.com